A Sunset Pictorial

Beautiful Hawaii

LANE MAGAZINE & BOOK COMPANY
MENLO PARK, CALIFORNIA

EDITED BY DOROTHY KRELL

DESIGN: JOHN FLACK
CARTOGRAPHY: BASIL C. WOOD

HAWAII EDITOR, *SUNSET* MAGAZINE: Nancy Bannick

Cover photographs: (front) Ke'e Beach, Kauai, by Tom Tracy; (back) red hibiscus by David Muench. Title page: Fern Jungle, Hawaii Volcanoes National Park, by David Muench.

Photographs by Ansel Adams on pages 111, 125, 172, and 223 are courtesy of the First National Bank of Hawaii. Photograph by Boone Morrison on page 171 is courtesy of the Hawaii State Foundation on Culture & The Arts; on page 179, courtesy of the Kauai Museum.

Contents

Preface

Hawaii has more than its share of natural beauty. Hawaii also has most of the same threats to the environment that we see around us on the mainland—plus additional threats unique to the Islands. The people of Hawaii have already done a great deal to cope with their problems. They are ahead of most mainland states in land-use controls and ahead of all mainland states in billboard controls. But Hawaii has much still to do to safeguard its environment.

We, the mainlanders, are part of Hawaii's problem. It could even be said that Hawaiian hospitality is one cause of Hawaii's problems. The aloha welcome and farewell keep luring us back.

Tourism is very important to Hawaii, but the people of Hawaii are learning the lessons we have been slow to learn on the mainland: ecology and natural beauty are fragile, irreplaceable; they must take precedence over "progress."

The beauty pictured in this book must be preserved for future generations. We assume that many who read this book have already visited the Islands and know the quality of the Hawaiian experience. It is our hope that increasing appreciation of the Islands will add support for their preservation.

Our purpose in this book is to show the beauties of Hawaii as accurately as we can. Exaggerated effects and photographic tricks we have left to others. We also assume that those who wish to study Hawaii's history and its socio-economic condition and future will look to excellent texts now available.

This book is an affectionate and respectful look at the natural attractions of our 50th state.

THE SUNSET EDITORS

An Introduction to Beautiful Hawaii

Some twenty-five million years ago, molten lava began to bubble up out of a fissure at the bottom of the sea. This was the beginning of the Hawaiian Ridge, the great range of volcanic mountains that today stretches for sixteen hundred miles across the Pacific Ocean just below the Tropic of Cancer. From ocean depths of more than 15,000 feet, the highest peaks rise above the surface of the sea to form the islands, islets, and atolls of the Hawaiian chain. Measured from the ocean floor, Mauna Kea on the island of Hawaii is the tallest mountain in the world, rising 13,796 feet above sea level and extending 19,680 feet below—a total of 33,476 feet.

Now once-bare lava slopes support gardens that blaze with bougainvillea, anthuriums, bird-of-paradise plants, orchids, hibiscus, and plumeria. Cattle range over cool grasslands below mountain summits that are tipped with snow in winter. Waterfalls spill from ginger-laden cliffs into clear, fern-banked pools. Billowing fields of sugar cane and neat rows of pineapple spread over thousands of fertile acres.

The major islands today are the eight that lie at the southeastern end of the chain. Seven of these are inhabited; the eighth, Kahoolawe, is used by the Navy for bombing and gunnery practice. Hawaii is the largest island—and is usually referred to as "the Big Island." With an area of 4,035 square miles, it is almost twice as large as all of the other Hawaiian Islands combined. The Big Island boasts two mountain peaks

PACIFIC OCEAN

Kauai
Lihue
Kaulakahi Channel
Niihau
Kauai Channel

Oahu
Kaneohe
Kailua
Honolulu
Kaiwi Channel

Molokai
Kaunakakai
Pailolo Channel

Lanai
Lahaina
Kahului
Maui
Hana
HALEAKALA
10,023

Kahoolawe
Alenuihaha Channel

N

Hawaii
MAUNA KEA
13,796
Hilo
Kailua
MAUNA LOA
13,680

Hawaiian Islands

"The loveliest fleet of islands that lies
anchored in any ocean." — Mark Twain.
Principal islands in the fleet are these eight
at the southeastern end of the chain.

that rise more than 13,000 feet from sea level, two active volcanoes, and a national park. Its varied climate and terrain provide great contrasts in scenery: sugar plantations, truck farms, cattle ranches, resorts, lush fern forests, orchards, flower fields, coffee plantations, and great expanses of lava.

Maui is the second largest island. It has some of the most magnificent beaches in Hawaii, a variety of resort areas, a refurbished whaling port, and the vast, colorful crater of dormant Haleakala.

West and northwest of Maui, the islands of Lanai and Molokai are quiet and comparatively undeveloped. Most of Lanai is owned by Dole Pineapple Company. Visitors are welcome, but tourist facilities are almost nonexistent. Much of Molokai is ranch land and pineapple fields, though resort development is in the beginning stages.

Oahu, third in size, is first in number of people. Honolulu, the state capital, is located here as are such famous landmarks as Diamond Head, Waikiki, and Pearl Harbor.

Westernmost of the main islands are Kauai and Niihau. Kauai is a mixture of sugar cane fields, resort areas, homes, and ranches. Lush vegetation blankets its mountains. Its volcanic summit, Waialeale, receives more than four hundred inches of rainfall annually and is reputed to be the wettest place on earth. Tiny Niihau is privately owned and can be visited only by special invitation. Its residents are mostly pure

Greeted by a fleet of double canoes manned by awed natives who welcomed him a god, Captain Cook sailed into Kealakekua Bay on January 17, 1779.

Hawaiians who live simply, without electricity, automobiles, or television.

Stretching beyond Niihau is a series of tiny islets and atolls officially named the Northwestern Hawaiian Islands but still commonly called the Leeward Islands. Volcanic activity began at this end of the chain. Kure and Midway are the oldest of the islands; Hawaii, where volcanic activity still continues, is the youngest. The islands at the northwest are estimated to be five to ten million years old, the main islands one to five million. Military installations on French Frigate Shoals, Midway, and Kure are the only marks of human habitation in the northwestern group.

The islands from Nihoa to Pearl and Hermes Reef comprise the Hawaiian Islands National Wildlife Refuge, established in 1909 to protect some of the most important sea bird nesting colonies in the world. Four endangered species of birds—the Laysan duck, Laysan finch, Nihoa finch, and Nihoa millerbird—are protected here, and the bare slopes and steep cliffs of these remote land bits are home to thousands of other birds. Also protected here are the rare Hawaiian monk seal and the green sea turtle.

The most generally accepted theory on the origins of the people who first settled in the Hawaiian Islands is that they came from Southeast Asia, following routes that took them down through the islands of Indonesia. From there they continued their migrations eastward to island dots in the vast Pacific. Eventually these early explorers reached all of the island groups in the Polynesian triangle formed by New Zealand at the southwest, Easter Island at the southeast, and the Hawaiian Islands at the north. It is thought that the first Polynesians to reach Hawaii sailed up from the

Marquesas about 750 A.D. Heavy migrations from Tahiti came later, during the twelfth and thirteenth centuries.

The voyagers traveled in huge double-hulled canoes, sixty to eighty feet long. A center platform between the hulls supported a thatched hut for shelter. They brought with them pigs, chickens, dogs, and plants that would provide food both during the long sea journey and in their new land. These early Hawaiians introduced many plants to the islands, including taro, which was their principal food crop, bananas, breadfruit, coconuts, sugar cane, yams, sweet potatoes, and mountain apples.

Somehow the islands of the Hawaiian archipelago eluded the European navigators of the sixteenth and seventeenth centuries. It was not until January 18, 1778, that English explorer Captain James Cook, on his third voyage in the Pacific, came upon the western end of the Hawaiian chain, sighting first Kauai, then Oahu, then Niihau. Cook made his first landing at Waimea on the island of Kauai. After a fortnight in the islands—which he named the Sandwich Islands in honor of his patron, the fourth Earl of Sandwich—he continued on to Alaska.

In November, Captain Cook returned to the tropical shores he had discovered earlier. This time he sighted Maui, Molokai, and lastly, the big island of Hawaii at the eastern end of the chain. On January 17, 1779, his two ships, the *Discovery* and the *Resolution,* sailed into Kealakekua Bay where the natives welcomed him as their god Lono, whose special celebration was held during the *makahiki,* or harvest, season—the time when Captain Cook chanced to appear.

Cook left the islands again on February 4 but soon returned after a sudden storm hit the ships off the coast of Kohala, collapsing the foremast of the *Resolution.* Ten days later, on February 14, the captain died at the edge of the bay—clubbed

Treated with great respect by the island priests, Captain Cook is draped with sacred red kapa in special ceremonies and presented with lavish offerings of food and gifts.

Feather image of Kukailimoku, fearsome war god of Kamehameha I. Images of this type, unique to Hawaii, were made by covering shaped basketry frame with netting to which feathers were attached.

BERNICE P. BISHOP MUSEUM

and stabbed to death during an altercation between his men and the natives, involving a cutter stolen from one of the ships.

The islands when Captain Cook arrived were divided into four kingdoms, each with a ruling chief. Wars were frequent among them. Kalaniopuu was chief of the island of Hawaii. His nephew, a young warrior from Kohala by the name of Kamehameha, was destined to become ruler of the entire island chain and the first of the eight monarchs that were to rule the island kingdom.

When the aging Kalaniopuu neared death, he named his highest-born son, Kiwalao, as his successor. To Kamehameha he gave the guardianship of the family war god, Kukailimoku. It was not long before strife developed between Kiwalao and Kamehameha. In a battle in 1782, Kiwalao was killed, but it took Kamehameha nine more years to gain control of all of the island of Hawaii. One by one, the other islands fell to Kamehameha. Early in 1795, he captured Maui, Lanai, and Molokai. In mid-April he landed his canoes at Waikiki on Oahu.

Victory over the Oahuans came after a bloody battle in which Kamehameha's forces drove the enemy inland and trapped them at the edge of the steep cliffs of Nuuanu Pali where many were killed and many more leaped to their deaths. Except for Kauai and Niihau, all of the islands were now under Kamehameha's rule. These came into his realm peacefully in April 1810 when Kaumualii, king of Kauai, entered into a pact with Kamehameha making Kauai a tributary kingdom in which Kaumualii would continue to govern Kauai but would accept Kamehameha's sovereignty.

For seventy-seven years, Kamehamehas ruled the island kingdom. Their reign ended on December 11, 1872, when Kamehameha V, a bachelor, died on the morning of his forty-third birthday. He left no heir to the throne and had named no successor. The next sovereign, William Lunalilo, was chosen by the Legislature. When he too died a bachelor, the Legislature elected David Kalakaua to rule the islands. Upon Kalakaua's death, his sister, Liliuokalani, took the throne. She reigned until the monarchy was overthrown on January 17, 1893. A Provisional Government then ruled the islands until the Republic of Hawaii was established on July 4, 1894.

As more and more foreigners landed in the islands, foreign intervention in Hawaiian affairs and rivalry for favors became extensive. Ships of England, France, Russia, and the United States made frequent visits to island ports, and Hawaii became a popular wintering place for ships en route to China with cargoes of furs collected during the summer along the Northwest coast of the U.S. mainland. Trade in sandalwood thrived from 1811 until the supply was exhausted in 1830. Then whaling took over as the mainstay of Hawaii's economy, and whaleships flocked to Hawaiian ports at Honolulu and Lahaina.

During the first half of the nineteenth century, a number of foreign powers made attempts to establish their positions in the islands. In 1816 the Russians erected a fort at Waimea on Kauai. The following year they were expelled by the king of Kauai under strict orders from Kamehameha. Protestant missionaries arrived in Hawaii from Boston in April of 1820 and began to teach the natives Christian principles, reading, writing, and arithmetic, and the rudiments of democracy. France's interest in the islands was expressed by the arrival of the first Roman Catholic missionaries from France in 1827. For five months in 1843, the islands were actually under the British flag after they were seized by a British naval officer, Lord George Paulet. The British government later disavowed Paulet's act, and the kingdom was returned to Kamehameha III.

Beginning in 1840, negotiations got under way to assure Hawaii's independence. On November 28, 1843, Britain and France signed a declaration recognizing the independence of the Hawaiian kingdom, and the following summer, the United States reaffirmed its recognition of Hawaii's independence.

Four whaling ships out of Nantucket are seen in this 1833 lithograph. During this period of history, about a hundred whalers visited Honolulu and Lahaina each year.

HAWAIIAN SUGAR PLANTERS' ASSN.

In the early 1880's, the narrow-gauge rail line above led from the Waimanalo Sugar Company mill on windward Oahu to Waimanalo Beach where cane was loaded aboard steamers for shipment to Honolulu. Below, in 1922, when Hawaiian Pineapple Company bought most of Lanai, draft animals were being used for field work.

DOLE COMPANY

The whaling industry, which reached its peak in 1852, went into a steady decline following the discovery of petroleum in Pennsylvania in 1859. Other misfortunes helped to bring about its demise, including a growing scarcity of whales and the losses of many whaling ships during the Civil War. The death blow to the industry came in 1871 when thirty-three ships, including seven of Hawaiian registry, were lost when they became trapped in Arctic ice north of Bering Strait.

Conversion to agriculture came about gradually. Sugar led the way—the top-ranking crop then as it is today. The first successful plantation was opened in 1835 at Koloa, Kauai. Other mills followed, and other crops were planted. The sugar industry expanded rapidly following the signing of a reciprocity treaty between Hawaii and the United States in 1875, permitting duty-free exchange of products between the two countries. Rice was grown to supply the needs of the Chinese. Coffee plantations were started on Kauai, Oahu, and on the Big Island. There were short-lived attempts to grow tobacco, cotton, wheat, potatoes, and to raise silkworms for a silk industry. Cattle ranches covered many acres of the Big Island and Maui. Some pineapple was grown, though the pineapple industry did not really get under way until the early 1900's after the Hawaiian Pineapple Company was organized by James D. Dole in 1901.

The mid-nineteenth century brought extensive growth in agriculture and trade in Hawaii. It also brought a shortage of laborers needed to work on the plantations. There simply were not enough Hawaiians to fill the need. In 1852 the first Chinese laborers were brought to the islands under five-year contracts. Other races followed—the first Japanese in 1868, Portuguese from Madeira and the Azores in 1878, Spanish in 1898, Koreans and Filipinos in the early 1900's. Some of these immigrants returned to their homelands after their contracts expired, but many stayed on in the islands. Some went into business for themselves. Many married Hawaiian women, and over the generations racial strains have become more and more complex. Since World War II about forty per cent of Hawaiian marriages have been inter-racial. Today pure Hawaiians and part Hawaiians make up only one sixth of the state's population. One fourth of Hawaii's people, are of mixed blood strains.

During the reign of Queen Liliuokalani, strong feelings grew among island businessmen favoring the annexation of Hawaii to the United States. The Spanish-American War finally convinced the United States government of the strategic position of the Hawaiian Islands in the Pacific and helped to turn the tide in favor of annexation. The sovereignty of the Republic was transferred in a ceremony at Iolani Palace at noon on August 12, 1898. However, it was not until almost two years later, on June 14, 1900, that the territorial government actually went into effect and Sanford B. Dole was appointed governor.

The struggle for statehood for Hawaii began as early as 1903. The first statehood bill was introduced in 1919, and others followed with regularity after that. Efforts at statehood were put aside during the tense period of World War II following Japan's surprise attack on Pearl Harbor on the morning of December 7, 1941. During the war years, Hawaii became America's defense post in the Pacific. Pearl Harbor was headquarters for the Pacific fleet, and Schofield Barracks was the largest Army post under the United States flag.

Efforts to gain statehood began again right after the war. But it was not until March 11, 1959, that Congress finally passed the enabling act. On August 21 of that year, President Dwight D. Eisenhower signed the proclamation that made the "Aloha State" the fiftieth star in the United States flag.

HONOLULU AND ENVIRONS...
A CITY GROWS,
SPREADS, MATURES

Waikiki Beach, left, was almost deserted in 1924, when the only two hotels were the Moana, shown here with its famous pier, and the Seaside, replaced in 1926 by the palatial Royal Hawaiian Hotel. Above, the trip over the twisting, wind-swept Nuuanu Pali Road in 1913 was a challenge to any touring buff. Polo was a crowd-pleaser at Kapiolani Park, below, when carriages rimmed the field in the early 1900's.

Three-masted sailing vessels crowd Honolulu Harbor in the 1888 scene above. Below, a mule-drawn tram car of Hawaiian Tramways, Ltd., stops in front of Aliiolani Hale on run from Houghtaling Road to Thomas Square. Electric trolleys replaced mule-cars in 1903.

Flags flutter from buildings along King Street on July 4, 1922. View is from the corner of Fort and King streets. Below, taro and rice, cultivated at Waipahu when this picture was taken in 1910, fed workers in Oahu Sugar Company's plantation town.

Oahu

Oahu is an island of tremendous variety, of famous views and unexpected ones, historic landmarks and modern architectural achievements, mushrooming towns and wilderness areas, windy heights and tropical valleys, and a fascinating melange of people and cultures. Its coastline offers magnificent seascapes, a varied assortment of beach parks, quiet coves, tide pools rich in marine life, and jagged, wave-lashed promontories. Hiking trails crisscross mountains that abound in splendid forests, unsurpassed scenery, waterfalls and swimming holes, and many native plants and birds. Colorful and friendly Honolulu, a sprawling city of more than 300,000 people, is a blend of South Seas, Orient, and modern American city, with a warmth and informality rarely seen on the mainland. Seat of Hawaiian government since 1850, it offers an intriguing look at Island history during monarchy, republic, territory, and statehood days. Honolulu Harbor, once a port of call for whalers and fur and sandalwood traders, now shelters luxury liners and freighters from around the world. At Waikiki, sun-bronzed bodies dot the sands of a modern resort center that was the seaside playground of early Hawaiian monarchs. Behind Honolulu, rain-washed valleys cut the purple-tinged Koolau Range that forms a mountain spine roughly paralleling the eastern shore of the island. Strong trade winds push through famous Nuuanu Pali, dramatic pass through the towering cliffs, and on the windward side of the mountains, suburban towns, farmland, lush pastures, and banana patches lie at the base of steep, green-clad ridges. To the west, the older Waianae Mountains slope up from a plateau planted to pineapple and sugar cane. On the ocean side of these mountains, broad, arid valleys open to sandy shores.

PHOTOGRAPH BY BOONE MORRISON

HONOLULU . . . ISLAND CAPITAL

Concrete towers house Hawaii's business giants, shoppers browse along
landscaped malls, and Honolulu Harbor bustles with the activity of a Pacific
crossroads; yet this modern American city retains delightful foreign
overtones and many reminders of a fascinating history.

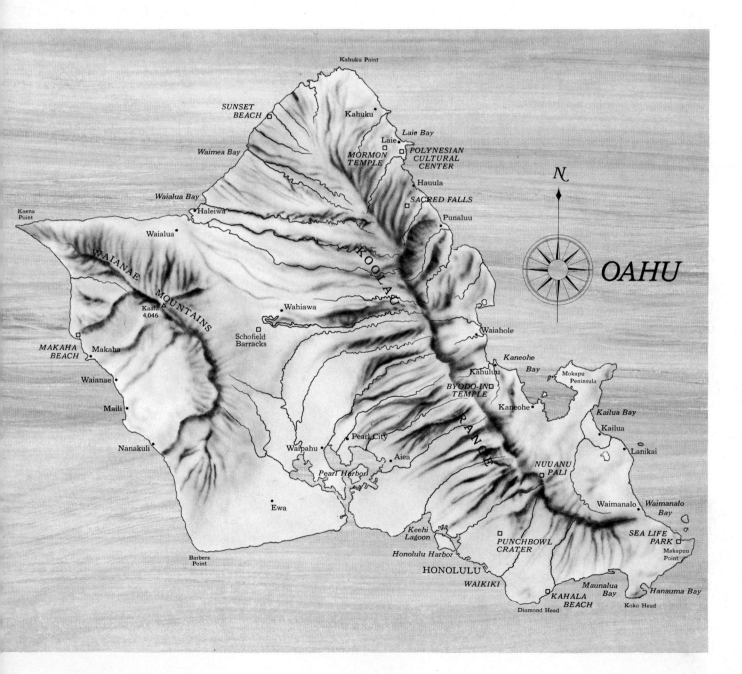

AN EVER-CHANGING SKYLINE and the familiar bulk of Diamond Head are
silhouetted against a cloud-splashed sky in this early-morning view from Magic
Island, thirty-two-acre peninsula off Ala Moana Park.

A HONOLULU LANDMARK since 1926, the 184-foot-high Aloha Tower stands at the foot of Fort Street, surrounded by passenger terminal and piers. An outdoor escalator connects the terminal's passenger deck with Irwin Park.

...HONOLULU

A SNUG HARBOR for ships since whaling days, Hawaii's major port is aptly named Honolulu, or "fair haven." Today's ship arrivals see these views of the downtown skyline. From piers adjacent to the Aloha Tower, the broad Ala Moana carries traffic past the business district and tree-shaded Ala Moana Park toward Waikiki.

THE CITY SPREADS over twenty-five miles of Oahu's leeward shore and inland onto the ridges and into the valleys of the Koolau Range. Waikiki, tourist playground, covers a peninsula that extends from Ala Wai Yacht Harbor (left in photo) to Diamond Head (just out of picture at right), bordered on one side by the ocean and on the inland side by the Ala Wai Canal.

TOM TRACY

OLD AND NEW are frequent neighbors in downtown Honolulu. Sleek new towers to house Hawaii's business giants seem to spring up almost overnight, but the efforts of concerned citizens are resulting in the saving of many architectural landmarks. On opposite page, the quaint 1870 facade of the former Kamehameha V Post Office (also shown at left) is in sharp contrast with Amfac's twenty-story glass and marble tower. Above, the 1881 home of the "Hawaiian Gazette" stands out against the volcanic aggregate and tinted bronze glass of the Financial Plaza of the Pacific.

BOONE MORRISON

ENJOYING NEW LIFE as restaurants, shops, and offices, some of Honolulu's oldest remaining commercial buildings have been carefully restored to fit their new roles. The two buildings on this page, at the corner of Merchant Street and Nuuanu Avenue, were built in the 1890's; both house restaurants.

BOONE MORRISON

DISTRICT COURT ANNEX now occupies the former quarters of the Yokohama Specie Bank, called the handsomest bank building in Honolulu when it was built in 1909.

...HONOLULU

KEITH GUNNAR

RICHARD ROWAN

THE WORKS OF MANY ARTISTS embellish business buildings, hotels, shopping centers, pedestrian malls. The bronze sculptured fountain above, by Bumpei Akaji, fronts the Bishop Trust Building. Columns at left, in Financial Plaza of the Pacific, are by Arnaldo Pomodoro. Graceful birds at right, by Kenneth Shutt, brighten entry to Kapiolani Branch of American Savings & Loan Association.

RICHARD ROWAN

TOM TRACY

SHOPPING CONTRASTS are great between modern centers such as Ala Moana (above), where outdoor escalators connect malls landscaped with fountains, sculptures, plants, and carp ponds, and the fascinating clutter and intriguing wares of Chinatown's shops and markets (right).

SUCH VARIED ENTERPRISES as restaurants, bars, night clubs, noodle factories, herb shops, bakeries, import shops, temples, and open-air markets contribute to the mood and bustle of Chinatown. Just wandering through this district bounded by Nuuanu Avenue, Beretania and River streets, and Nimitz Highway can be an adventure.

GLENN CHRISTIANSEN

IMPRESSIVE STATE CAPITOL is viewed here from lanai of Iolani Palace. Open to the sky and to Island breezes, the building has a feeling of spaciousness and light. An Island theme dominates both interior and exterior. Conical legislative chambers represent the volcanoes that formed Hawaii; graceful 60-foot columns are patterned after royal palms; Molokai sand was used in court paving, koa wood in interior trim and furnishings.

A. SALBOSA

GLENN CHRISTIANSEN

OPEN CROWN of capitol is formed by 36 cantilevered concrete ribs with glass mosaic tiles between. From the fifth floor, visitors can look down into the central court and out to views of city, sea, and mountains. Passageways from central court lead to reflecting pools, left, on which the building appears to float.

OPENING OF LEGISLATURE in January is a
colorful, festive event. Lavish bouquets
crowd the desks; leis are heaped on lawmakers'
shoulders; musicians, singers, and hula
dancers entertain; and an intent audience
watches the proceedings.

PHOTOGRAPHS BY A. SALBOSA

HONOLULU'S PAST is brought to life in restored architectural treasures in the Civic Center. Missionaries from New England established the first Honolulu mission here in 1820 and built the Islands' first frame house (above) the following year from materials shipped around the Horn. Nearby Kawaiahao Church (left) was dedicated in 1842. The coral block structure was preceded by four thatched churches.

OAHU **41**

. . . HONOLULU

CORONATION PAVILION, built in 1883 for ceremonies in which King Kalakaua crowned himself and Queen Kapiolani, is now the setting for Friday lunch-hour concerts by the Royal Hawaiian Band. Dome is original; termite-damaged foundation and pillars have been rebuilt of concrete. Eight pillars represent the eight major islands; shields are designs based on various flags.

ONLY ROYAL PALACE in the United States, Iolani Palace was completed in 1882 for King Kalakaua and occupied by him, then by his sister and successor to the throne, Queen Liliuokalani, until the monarchy was overthrown in 1893.

. . . HONOLULU

AN ISLAND OF QUIET in the midst of the downtown bustle, Thomas Square is a tree-shaded, grassy link between the lovely, tile-roofed Honolulu Academy of Arts (above) and the impressive Honolulu International Center (right). Displayed in galleries around attractively landscaped courtyards in the Academy of Arts building are world-recognized masterpieces, contemporary exhibits, and the works of outstanding Hawaiian artists. The arch-fronted concert hall at right is part of a complex that also includes a sports arena, exhibition and assembly halls, and meeting rooms.

A. SALBOSA

KAMEHAMEHA DAY PARADE on June 11 is part of a celebration honoring the ruler who unified the Islands. Island blossoms decorate the colorful floats, and Kamehameha's statue in front of the Judiciary Building is draped with 40-foot leis for the occasion.

A. SALBOSA

HAWAII'S UNIQUE HERITAGE
is not forgotten. Many cultures,
ethnic backgrounds, and
historical events helped to shape
the island state, and these ties
with the past are preserved in many
special celebrations. Philippine
folk dancers above are a feature
of the month-long Fiesta Filipina;
at right, kimono-clad dancers of all
ages join in Japanese Bon Dances.

WALTON WIMBERLY

ORIENTAL ARCHITECTURE is a colorful addition to the city scene. The First Chinese Church of Christ was established by thirty-six Christian Chinese immigrants in 1879. The building above, which combines Western and Oriental influences, is its second home, dedicated in 1929. Glazed tile work surrounds its handsome entry door.

. . . HONOLULU

IZUMO TAISHAKYO MISSION was built without nails in 1923 by a master shrine carpenter brought from Japan for the job. It became the property of the city during World War II, later was regained by the Shinto members and rebuilt on this site facing Nuuanu Stream. Though modified to fit modern building codes, the temple retains many of its original features.

DAVID CORNWELL

... HONOLULU

HAWAII'S PARKS AND GARDENS are a joy to gardeners and non-gardeners alike. The tranquil Japanese garden at left borders Manoa Stream at the East-West Center. The stream flows down three levels, symbolizing mountains, plains, and sea. Below, yellow rainbow shower trees around Louise Dillingham Memorial Fountain in Kapiolani Park are a colorful spectacle in May and June.

ARCHING BRANCHES of huge banyan tree provide a shady canopy in Kapiolani Park. These enormous trees spread from thick central trunks. Aerial roots that drop from the main branches grow into supporting secondary trunks.

A. SALBOSA

A. SALBOSA

NOTEWORTHY DISPLAYS of color and rare plant material reward the visitor to these two sites. Along the Pali Highway, the poinsettia hedge at left is a riot of crimson bloom from December to March. Rare exotic plants, magnificent trees, and outstanding orchids, bromeliads, and palms are among the special collections in Foster Botanic Garden, above.

HONOLULU'S HEIGHTS AND VALLEYS

The city climbs the ridges and spills into the mist-laden valleys
that stretch up to the cloud-topped peaks of the Koolau Range.

*HILL OF SACRIFICE, or Puowaina, is Hawaiian name for Punchbowl Crater (above), where row
upon row of simple tablets mark the graves of some 22,000 war dead in the National Memorial
Cemetery of the Pacific. The Chinese cemetery at right covers a green hillside in Manoa Valley.*

AN UNDISTURBED COUNTRYSIDE with stream, petroglyphs, and many species of native plants lies at Honolulu's northwestern edge. Princess Bernice Pauahi Bishop, last descendant of Kamehameha the Great and heiress to the Kamehameha lands, willed lovely, uninhabited Moanalua Valley to Samuel M. Damon in 1884. Hikers can get permission from the Damon Estate in Honolulu to walk the valley's trails.

. . . HEIGHTS AND VALLEYS

HIGHEST AND COOLEST of Honolulu's residential areas spreads up the slope of Tantalus, volcanic peak that rises above the central city. Here beautiful homes are almost hidden in lush vegetation, and panoramic views appear at many a turn. The city takes on a soft sunset glow in this view from Puu Ualakaa State Park.

TOM TRACY

BOONE MORRISON

HAWAII HALL, first permanent classroom building on the University of Hawaii's Manoa Valley campus, was completed in time for the 1912-1913 school year. Other "old campus" buildings were of similar columned, tile-roofed design. Figure used in design on Varney Circle fountain in foreground is a composite of Hawaiian gods.

EAST-WEST CENTER

GLENN CHRISTIANSEN

*EAST-WEST CENTER shares University of
Hawaii campus. It was established in 1960
to promote cultural and technical
interchange among peoples of Asia, the
Pacific, and the United States. The Center
is supported by government appropriations
and administered in cooperation with
the University.*

WAIKIKI . . . CITY WITHIN A CITY

Crowded and colorful, Waikiki is where the action is. Honolulu's visitor headquarters is this peninsula that was once a swamp with taro fields.

HIGH-RISE HOTELS and business buildings tower high above the palms that border Kalakaua Avenue. On the ocean side, balconies provide a dizzying view of the beach below.

. . . WAIKIKI

SURFERS RIDE WAIKIKI'S WAVES,
catamarans and outriggers deck the
horizon, sun-bronzed bodies cover the
narrow strand, youngsters play in the
reef-protected waters, and people
watching is at its best.

OAHU'S SHORE . . . ITS ATTRACTIONS ARE VARIED

Superb seascapes, romantic beaches, and a wealth of marine life are waiting to be enjoyed at the edge of the sea.

AN ASTONISHING WORLD of marine life surrounds the Hawaiian Islands. Amateurs and experts alike study the sea's treasures. The kindergarten class at left is collecting tide pool specimens for their salt-water aquarium. More professional studies are made at Sea Life Park (above and right), where shows are based on marine biologists' research into whale and porpoise behavior, and exhibits simulate the offshore marine environment and explain the exciting experiments being conducted at adjacent Oceanic Institute and the Makai Undersea Test Range.

DAVID MUENCH

THOR SVENSON

FISHING IS A FAVORITE PASTIME on all of the Islands, and on almost every rocky point or sandy beach, you will usually see someone dunking a line or tossing a net. The offshore waters are lucrative hunting grounds for spear fishermen.

DAVID MUENCH

BIG WAVES AND BEACH PARKS are two attractions of the dry Waianae Coast. Valleys
are hemmed in by parched cliffs, and the lowlands are scrubby with lantana, cactus,
and kiawe. This driest part of the island, in the lee of the Waianae Mountains is
fast developing as a tourist and residential area. Above, kiawes edge the sand along
the Makua shore; at right, waves pound a rocky point near Makaha.

. . . OAHU'S SHORE

THROUGH AND OVER THE MOUNTAINS

Today two freeways tunnel through the Koolau cliffs, but the old cross-island trail used by early Hawaiians is still there.

TWIN TUNNELS of the Pali Highway pierce the Koolaus. Above the freeway, part of the old cross-island road winds along the windward cliff below Pali Lookout. Originally an old Hawaiian footpath, it was improved for horses in 1845, later widened for carriages, still later for cars. At right, Nuuanu Pali Drive twists through a forest of eucalyptus, hau, bamboo, ti, ginger, and philodendron.

FROM PALI LOOKOUT the breathtaking view is northward along the fluted windward palisades to Mololii, small island at the tip of Kaneohe Bay, and out to Mokapu Peninsula at the bay's southeastern end. Below the Lookout are the greens of pastures, farms, cemetery, golf course. It was over this sheer precipice that Kamehameha the Great forced some of Oahu's warriors when he conquered the island in 1795.

MARTIN LITTON

LIKELIKE HIGHWAY descends from Wilson Tunnel through banana farms along the base of the green cliffs on the windward side of the Koolaus.

...OVER THE MOUNTAINS

IN A BEAUTIFUL SETTING, with a backdrop of nearly vertical cliffs, the eighteen-hole Pali Golf Course is just about thirty minutes from Waikiki. Hawaii's golfers can tee off by the sea or on volcanic slopes on a variety of courses that offer almost ideal conditions for year-round play.

BOONE MORRISON

AROUND THE KOOLAUS

Suburban communities and beach parks cluster alongside bays, farms and pastures reach deep into green valleys, and just an hour or so from Honolulu are country towns that have changed little in half a century.

THE VALLEY OF THE TEMPLES features the above replica of Byodo-In Temple, 900-year-old Buddhist temple in Japan. Hundreds of brilliantly hued carp (opposite), called koi by the Japanese, enliven its one-acre reflecting pond. Bred in Japan over many centuries from plain gray carp, these colorful fish, seen in landscape pools throughout Hawaii, are beloved pets and valuable possessions. To the Japanese, they symbolize manliness and courage and are said to bring good luck.

ROY KRELL

DAVID
CORNWELL

...AROUND THE KOOLAUS

ON THE WINDWARD SIDE of the mountains, a water buffalo grazes contentedly just a few minutes away from suburban settlements, and farmers tend crops that will supply Island markets.

...AROUND THE KOOLAUS

HANDICRAFTS, MUSIC, AND DANCES of Polynesia are demonstrated in the six villages of the Polynesian Cultural Center. Islanders from Tahiti, Tonga, Fiji, Samoa, and Hawaii, and New Zealand's Maori tell visitors about the cultures of their homelands. Above, visitors line lagoon to watch the colorful "Pageant of the Long Canoes," water-borne show presented daily.

PHOTOGRAPHS BY RICHARD ROWAN

WINDSWEPT LAIE POINT juts into the sea north of Hauula. About six thousand acres in the Laie area have been a development project of the Mormon Church since 1864. They include the town of Laie, the Polynesian Cultural Center, the Church College of Hawaii, and the landmark Mormon Temple (opposite).

...AROUND THE KOOLAUS

THE EASY PACE OF OLD HAWAII is still felt on the North Shore. Small boats find a protected moorage beneath the trees that overhang the banks of picturesque Anahulu Stream at Haleiwa, where missionaries settled in 1832.

...AROUND THE KOOLAUS

CALM, SHALLOW WATERS off Haleiwa Beach Park are ideal for youngsters' sand building. The cove is protected by Waialua Bay's long rock breakwater. In the distance, the Waianae Mountains rise behind Haleiwa town.

...AROUND THE KOOLAUS

AWESOME BREAKERS build up in winter off north and west side beaches. Waves like this one that tower up dramatically and crash forward with frightening violence challenge the experts in Hawaii surfing competitions, but for the average surfer, the ideal wave is a gentler one that breaks far out and gives a long ride. The surfer catches the wave just as the crest begins to spill over, then slides diagonally across the face just ahead of the breaking foam.

THOR SVENSON

STORM CLOUDS shadow the forested Waianae Mountains in this view from Haleiwa. The Waianaes are outdoorsmen's territory. The few roads that climb them are private or under military restriction. On the dry leeward side of the mountains are broad valleys and splendid beaches. To windward, pineapple fields spread over fertile Schofield plateau.

...AROUND THE KOOLAUS

LILIUOKALANI CHURCH, below, fifth to be built on the site of the North Shore's first mission, has ancient bell, memorial archway, and clock presented by Queen Liliuokalani in 1890.

Hawaii

Clouds brush the summits of Mauna Kea and Mauna Loa, the huge mountains that
dominate the Big Island. Between mountain peaks and sea lie rain forests, weird lava
formations, fertile grasslands, colorful gardens, orchards and truck farms, sugar and
coffee plantations, and cattle ranches. The Neighbor Islands' largest town, Hilo, sprawls
alongside crescent-shaped Hilo Bay, while in the northwest corner of the island, a
remarkably untouched bit of Hawaii survives in North Kohala, birthplace and boyhood
home of the first Kamehameha. Up on the cool Waimea plateau, mists swirl over
forest-capped hills and green grazing land. A few miles away, developers are at work
on resort complexes along a dry, sunny coast. In beautiful, isolated valleys on the
northeast coast, a luxuriant growth of native plants and trees is watered by abundant
year-round rainfall and streams fed by the winter snows that frequently dust Mauna
Kea's summit. This big island, youngest in the Hawaiian chain, is still growing. Of the
five volcanoes that formed Hawaii, two are still active. Kilauea and the summit caldera
and northeast flank of Mauna Loa are part of Hawaii Volcanoes National Park, which
is also a place to see rain forests, rare plants and native birds, and ancient Hawaiian
ruins. Mauna Loa, largest active volcano in the world, has not erupted since 1950.
But lively Kilauea, down on its southeast flank, puts on frequent fiery shows,
occasionally sending lava spilling all the way to the sea and adding more land area
to an island that is already almost twice as large as all of the other islands combined.

PHOTOGRAPH BY BOONE MORRISON

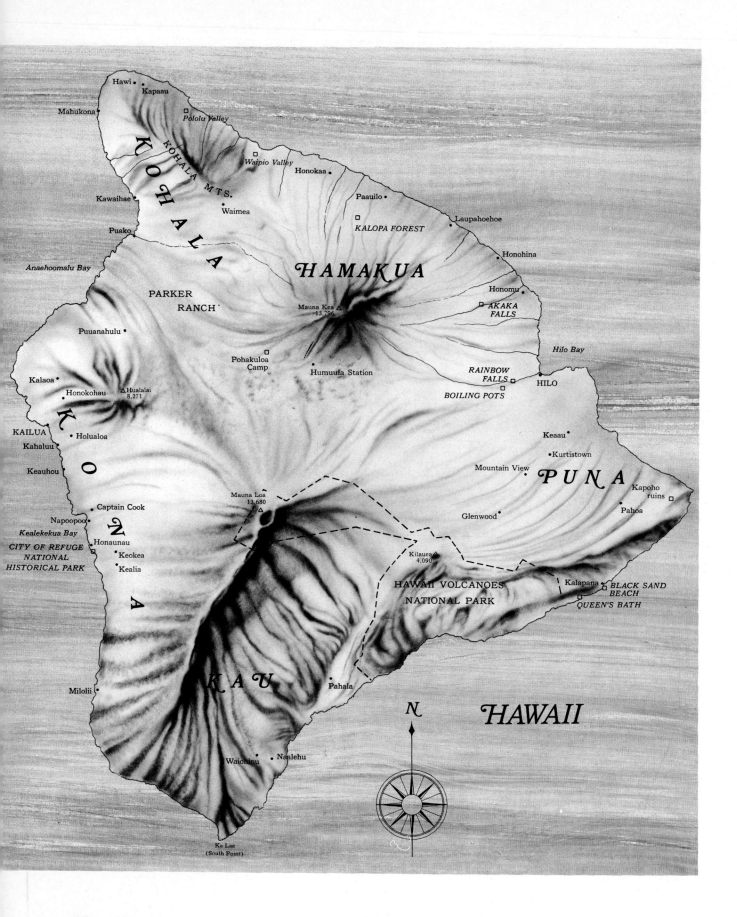

Hawi
Kapaau
Mahukona
□ Pololu Valley
Waipio Valley
KOHALA MTS.
Honokaa
Kawaihae
Waimea
Paauilo
Puako
□ KALOPA FOREST
Laupahoehoe
Anaehoomalu Bay
HAMAKUA
Honohina
PARKER
RANCH
Honomu
Puuanahulu
Mauna Kea
△
13,796
□ AKAKA
FALLS
Pohakuloa
Camp
Hilo Bay
Kalaoa
Honokohau
△ Hualalai
8,271
Humuula Station
RAINBOW
FALLS □
BOILING POTS
HILO
KAILUA
Holualoa
Keaau
Kahaluu
Kurtistown
Keauhou
Mountain View
PUNA
K O N A
Mauna Loa
13,680
△
Kapoho
ruins □
Captain Cook
Glenwood
Pahoa
Napoopoo
Kealekekua Bay
Honaunau
CITY OF REFUGE
NATIONAL
HISTORICAL PARK
Keokea
Kealia
Kilauea △
4,090
HAWAII VOLCANOES
NATIONAL PARK
Kalapana
□ BLACK SAND
BEACH
QUEEN'S BATH
K A U
Milolii
Pahala
N
HAWAII
Waiohinu
Naalehu
Ka Lae
(South Point)

N

HILO . . . A CITY SHAPED BY WATER

Rivers, lagoons, and waterfalls are scenic attractions, and a magnificent green belt now serves Hiloans along a waterfront where two tsunamis wreaked havoc.

*LILIUOKALANI GARDENS cover almost thirty acres of Hilo's Waiakea Peninsula.
Hit hard by disastrous seismic waves in 1946 and 1960, Hilo has rebuilt its
waterfront to include well-tended plantings, ponds and lagoons, and a bayside drive.*

. . . HILO

HILO BAY forms a great arc at the edge of the Neighbor Islands' largest town, which stretches along the waterfront and up green slopes to 1,500 feet. In the foreground is Waiakea Peninsula. Tree-shaded areas along waterfront are popular picnic spots.

*CATAMARAN from a nearby hotel glides quietly past old diving
structure at tip of Coconut Island on a sunset sail around Hilo Bay.*

...HILO

SAMPAN HARBOR at mouth of Wailoa River shelters a good-sized fishing fleet. Spirited bidding takes place when the catch is auctioned in the early morning.

BOONE MORRISON

RICHARD ROWAN

HILO WATER BABY leads a happy life. Youngsters here grow up in and around the water and can paddle about in tidal pools and coves at the east end of town.

HILOANS, like most Hawaiians, love to fish, and there's always an admiring audience when a big one is about to be landed.

BOONE MORRISON

NORTH OF HILO . . . JUNGLED GORGES, GRASSY PARKS

Stream-eroded gulches are lush with gingers, ferns, ti, azaleas, orchids, and bamboo. Detours lead to country towns, grassy parks, wave-battered bluffs.

TOM TRACY

A COOL, GREEN JUNGLE cloaks the gorge cut by Kolekole Stream. Lush foliage canopies the path that loops through Akaka Falls State Park. Streams and waterfalls cascade through thick tropical vegetation. Akaka Falls (right) drops in a silvery plume over a 442-foot precipice to Kolekole Stream.

DAVID MUENCH

BOONE MORRISON

A GRASSY PARKLAND borders Kalopa Gulch. A state recreation area here offers trails and picnic sites and protects a 100-acre stand of mature native and introduced trees.

LAUPAHOEHOE PENINSULA is a tranquil scene in these pictures. Its pleasant, grassy park is popular with campers and picnickers. But tragedy struck here in 1946 when a powerful tsunami swept over the tiny settlement that occupied the peninsula. A monument to the victims stands near the site of a school that was demolished in the disaster. Twenty-four names, mostly of students and teachers, appear on the marker.

JUNGLED GORGES cut the northeastern slope of Mauna Kea where the trade winds drop heavy rainfall. Canyons here are laced with waterfalls and lush with tropical vegetation.

100 HAWAII

...NORTH OF HILO

THE FULL FORCE OF THE SEA strikes this windward coast. With no offshore reef to break the onslaught, ocean swells splash unchecked against the jagged lava rocks.

PUNA . . . GARDENS, ORCHARDS, BLACK SAND BEACHES

Cinder cones and stark black lava contrast strikingly with fields of delicate vanda orchids and thriving orchards of papayas and macadamias.

ORCHIDS FLOURISH at the base of a huge cinder cone formed in 1960 when a spectacular eruption took place along Kilauea's east rift zone. Big Island orchid growers ship some thirty million orchid blossoms each year.

BOONE MORRISON

A VILLAGE WAS BURIED beneath the cinders that spewed from 420-foot Kapoho cone in 1960. Seventy homes were buried beneath the lava. Today the highway passes right over what was once Kapoho town. In this eruption, the state's easternmost point was extended about 500 feet closer to California.

...PUNA

PAPAYAS, among the most popular of Island fruits, are grown commercially in Puna. During the past ten years, their crop value has increased three-fold.

MACADAMIA NUT TREES stretch almost to the sea in this commercial orchard south of Hilo. The trees produce an extremely hard-shelled nut which is opened by a special cracking machine. Papayas, macadamia nuts, and Island flowers lead the way toward diversification and expansion of Hawaii's agricultural base.

GLENN CHRISTIANSEN

GLENN CHRISTIANSEN

CRYSTAL CLEAR Queen's Bath, a natural pool in a large lava crack near Kalapana, is a favorite swimming hole for local youngsters.

SCULPTURED BY THE ELEMENTS, Puna's lava bluffs are constantly changing. In time, the ocean may cut this section off completely.

A TREASURE HOUSE of painting, trim little Star of the Sea Church at Kalapana is a picture postcard inside and out. Subtle colors depict Biblical scenes on ceiling and walls, windows have painted-on canopies, and painted-on columns appear to support the barrel-vaulted ceiling. A Belgian priest completed the initial decoration in 1929; additional touches, such as the painted entry door, were added in 1963-64 by another artist.

BOONE MORRISON

SMOOTHED BY A FROTH of white foam and fringed by graceful palms, Kaimu Black Sand Beach is a striking study in contrasts. The black sand was formed when lava hit the sea and exploded into bits and then was ground finer by the action of the surf.

ANTHURIUMS thrive in the delicate shade cover given by tree ferns. The waxy blooms rank number one in Big Island flower sales.

HAWAII **109**

DAVID MUENCH

VOLCANOES . . . FAMOUS BIG ISLAND ATTRACTION

The lava can flow at any time on this island where Pele, the restless volcano goddess, has made her home.

STEAM BILLOWS from bluffs and ground cracks at many places around Kilauea caldera and along the Chain of Craters Road. It is formed when ground water seeps into hot areas beneath the surface.

AA AND PAHOEHOE, Hawaiian words
for the two types of lava found in
the Islands, are now universally used
by geologists to describe lavas
throughout the world. Aa (right) is
rough and chunky; pahoehoe (below)
is smooth, ropy, or billowy.

AN AWESOME SIGHT during a time of volcanic activity, fountains of fire, which have reached hundreds of feet, illuminate Halemaumau's lava walls, and a pool of molten lava bubbles on the crater floor. The night scene above was photographed during a lively 1968 outbreak.

GLENN CHRISTIANSEN

THURSTON LAVA TUBE was formed when the outer crust of a lava flow hardened while the molten river of lava within continued to move. Early Hawaiians used similar tubes as burial caves.

. . . VOLCANOES

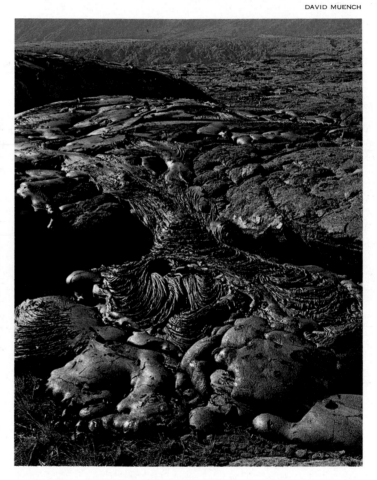

FERNS AND LICHEN appear early on lava flows. Where rainfall is light, lava remains almost bare for years.

A TOE OF PAHOEHOE from a new flow cools atop an older flow where plant life has begun.

A STEAMING HALEMAUMAU is viewed across the scarred floor of Kilauea caldera.

DAVID MUENCH

A LIFELESS LANDSCAPE borders the Devastation Trail, a half-mile-long boardwalk that crosses a deep carpet of pumice through a skeleton forest of dead ohias. A 1959 eruption in Kilauea Iki (Little Kilauea) rained cinders on this region.

A FERN JUNGLE on the east side of Kilauea Iki contrasts with the bleak scene opposite. Giant tree ferns up to twenty feet tall and other smaller ferns grow beneath a tangle of weathered ohia trees.

AROUND THE SOUTHERN TIP

Fishermen of today and yesterday have been bountifully rewarded off the Big Island's southern shore; and at the island's southernmost tip, archeologists have found remnants of Hawaii's oldest known civilization.

DAVID CORNWELL

SOUTHERNMOST TIP of land in the United States is uninhabited now, but traces of civilization dating back to about 750 A.D. have been unearthed at South Point. The stone wall pictured at left is the remains of an early heiau.

TOM TRACY

OUTRIGGERS on Milolii's coral-and-lava beach are powered by outboard motors today, but otherwise the scene has changed little over the years. The day's catch is trucked to Hilo's auction.

CANOE-MOORING HOLES at South Point were chipped in the rocks by early
Hawaiians who secured their canoes by running the bowlines through these rings.
Fishing is outstanding where currents meet off this wind-lashed point.

KONA ... MODERN RESORTS AND OLD HAWAII

Visitors to Kona can shop, try restaurants and night spots, cool off in hotel pools, and visit historic and scenic treasures that are reminders of a different Hawaii.

BOONE MORRISON

KAILUA'S WATERFRONT is a popular gathering place. A pedestrian walkway borders the curving sea wall where fishermen of all ages try their luck.

A PALACE AND THE ISLANDS' OLDEST CHURCH lie just a few steps apart in Kailua. Gracious Hulihee Palace, built in 1837-38 by Hawaii's governor, Kuakini, served as King Kalakaua's summer palace in the 1880's. Behind it is Mokuaikaua Church, built in 1837 by the first missionaries.

. . . KONA

TOURIST KONA is Kailua village and thereabouts. The fisherman at right caught his first marlin after a two-hour fight. The tag shows its weight—661 pounds. Open-air shop below, with its barefoot salesgirl, offers a typical miscellany of colorful wares.

GLENN CHRISTIANSEN

RICHARD ROWAN

TOURISTS ARE TEMPTED
by a wide selection of
merchandise ranging from shells
and coral offered by young
entrepreneurs along Kailua's sea
wall to elegant resort wear
and imported curios in
the local shops.

TOWERING FIGURES at Honaunau's restored City of Refuge are
reproductions of ancient wooden images. This was the highest ranking
of the refuges that once stood in every major district in the Islands.

TOM TRACY

CITY OF REFUGE was a haven
for defeated warriors, noncombatants,
and lawbreakers for four hundred
years. Thatch structure on point is a
reconstruction of Hale-o-Keawe, which
became the main temple after 1650
and the tomb of twenty-three chiefs.
Its wooden framework shows in half-size
model (below) displayed in the park.
The Great Wall, which encloses refuge
on landward side, is of lava boulders
fitted together without mortar.

RICHARD ROWAN

ANSEL ADAMS

ONLY COFFEE INDUSTRY in the nation thrives in the cool uphill section of Kona,
where plants are shaded by a dependable afternoon cloud cover and nourished by
rich volcanic soil. Most beans are dried mechanically today, but at Kona's largest mill,
some are still sun-dried in this large shed with rollaway roof.

... KONA

COFFEE "CHERRIES" ripen unevenly on stem, and each berry must be picked at exactly the right moment. Mechanical picker, which shakes ripe berries from plant, is in use now, but on small family farms, youngsters often help with the picking.

KONA'S CHURCHES are picturesque landmarks. St. Benedict's Church, above and left, has charming exterior, hand-painted murals and decorative designs on interior walls, ceiling, and pillars. Decorated by a Belgian priest about 1900, it is known as "the Painted Church."

DAVID CORNWELL

ST. PETER'S CATHOLIC CHURCH is a much-photographed landmark at the edge of Kahaluu Bay. The tiny blue-and-white structure was built on a heiau site to overcome superstition.

KOHALA IS A REGION OF CONTRASTS

Verdant grasslands cloak the slopes of the mile-high Kohala Mountains; tourists bask on a sun-baked coast; and beautiful, remote valleys cut the windward face of the island's oldest volcano.

DAVID CORNWELL

ON A WINDSWEPT PLATEAU, backed by the green-carpeted Kohala Mountains and Mauna Kea's often snow-topped summit, Parker Ranch lands spread over almost a quarter of a million acres of the Big Island. The air is cool here at 2,500 feet, but a sun-baked coast is only minutes away.

CATTLE first arrived in Hawaii in 1793, when Captain Vancouver presented a small herd to Kamehameha, who turned them loose to multiply. Twenty years later, seaman John Palmer Parker left his ship to round up wild cattle for the king. He developed a domestic herd from captured stock and acquired land to start the now-famous Parker Ranch. Hawaiian cowboys are still called "paniolos," the name given to cowboys brought from Latin America to teach riding and roping.

. . . KOHALA

BEAUTIFUL VALLEYS, laced with waterfalls and resplendent with native plants, cut the windward face of the Kohala Mountains. Waipio Valley, above, is accessible by trail or by four-wheel-drive vehicle.

THREE HIKERS follow trail behind Kapoloa Falls, which drop down a sheer cliff in Pololu Valley along Kohala's northeast coast.

HAWAII **133**

POWDERY BEACHES edge a kiawe-covered shore along the South Kohala coast.
The curve of Kaunaoa Beach, above, is backed by a luxury hotel and golf course. In the
distance, Mauna Kea, often snow-capped, slopes up to almost 14,000 feet from sea level.

... KOHALA

PETROGLYPHS in lava near Puako were carved by early Hawaiians. Puukohola Heiau, below, south of Kawaiahae, was the last sacrificial temple built by Kamehameha the Great.

135

ATOP THE HIGHEST MOUNTAINS

The Saddle Road crosses a lonely, lava-blanketed pass between Mauna Kea
and Mauna Loa, highest and second highest peaks in the Hawaiian archipelago.

*ON THE BLEAK UPPER SLOPES of Mauna Kea, a cinder road climbs to observatories at 13,780 feet,
where scientists conduct astronomical studies in clear air far removed from population centers.*

*FROM MAUNA KEA'S SLOPES,
Mauna Loa, across the saddle,
appears deceptively close.
Its summit is actually almost
thirty miles away.*

Maui

Maui has a slogan "Maui no ka oi," which translates "Maui is the best," and a fast-growing number of residents and returning visitors seem to agree with the claim. The second largest island in the Hawaiian chain began its existence as two separate land masses, formed by volcanic activity at different times. First to appear were the West Maui Mountains, which slope up to a summit that is the second rainiest peak in Hawaii. The rounded dome of mighty Haleakala rose as a separate island to the southeast. The isthmus that joins them today was formed by centuries of erosion from their slopes and is the reason for Maui's present nickname, the Valley Island. Today fields of sugar cane blanket the fertile plain, and sugar cane and pineapple cover the foothills. Along the sunny coast of West Maui, luxurious resorts, condominiums, golf courses, shopping complexes, and residential communities share the scene with palm-fringed beaches and restored historic landmarks that bring to life the lusty days when whalers wintered in Hawaiian ports. Windward slopes of the mountains are cut by jungled valleys laced with sparkling streams and beautiful with tropical foliage and picturesque waterfalls. A twisting road hugs weathered bluffs above ferny gulches on Haleakala's north side to reach the eastern end of Maui, where the easy pace and quiet charm of Hana is reminiscent of early Island life. Kiawe-covered shores edge secluded bays in the lee of Haleakala. Up on the slopes, cool grasslands are quiet grazing grounds for ranch animals, and vegetables and flowers are grown for Island markets, and at the very top of the mountain, the sun paints delicate colors on the lava cones inside a crater almost large enough to hold Manhattan Island.

PHOTOGRAPH BY BOONE MORRISON

MAUI . . . THE VALLEY ISLE

A low-lying isthmus now unites two volcanic masses that were once separate islands and gives Maui its nickname, the "Valley Isle."

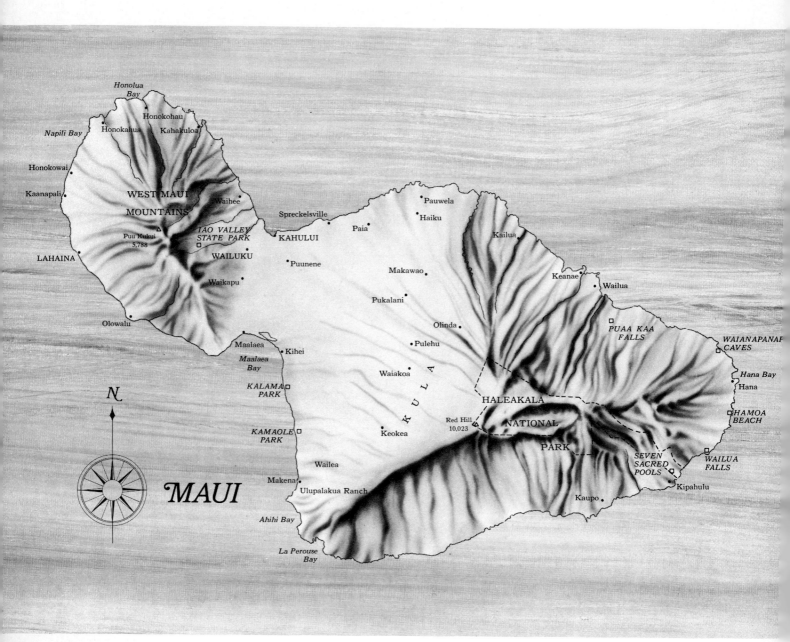

Honolua Bay
Honokohau
Napili Bay
Honokahua
Kahakuloa
Honokowai
Kaanapali
WEST MAUI MOUNTAINS
Waihee
Spreckelsville
Pauwela
Haiku
Paia
Kailua
Puu Kukui 5,788
IAO VALLEY STATE PARK
KAHULUI
LAHAINA
WAILUKU
Puunene
Makawao
Keanae
Wailua
Waikapu
Pukalani
Olowalu
Olinda
PUAA KAA FALLS
WAIANAPANAPA CAVES
Maalaea
Kihei
Pulehu
Hana Bay
Maalaea Bay
Waiakoa
K U L A
Hana
KALAMA PARK
HALEAKALA
HAMOA BEACH
KAMAOLE PARK
Red Hill 10,023
NATIONAL
Keokea
PARK
SEVEN SACRED POOLS
WAILUA FALLS
Wailea
Makena
Ulupalakua Ranch
Kaupo
Kipahulu
Ahihi Bay
La Perouse Bay

N

MAUI

ONCE SEPARATED BY WATER, Haleakala and the West Maui Mountains are now joined by a seven-mile-wide isthmus formed by erosion from their slopes. Maalaea Bay lies at the southwest end of the plain (left in photo), Kahului Harbor at the northeast.

141

GREEN-CLAD WALLS of Iao Valley, left, cut into the center of Puu Kukui, second rainiest peak in Hawaii. Above, Iao Needle, a 2,250-foot-high pinnacle, juts up from the floor of the hushed, often cloud-draped ravine.

MOUNTAIN WATCHING is as fascinating as wave watching from Maui's beaches. Across Maalaea Bay, above, all of Haleakala sometimes appears sparkling clear; at other times, its upper slopes are lost in a swirl of clouds. At right, the West Maui Mountains add to the view from H. A. Baldwin Park. The friendly dogs are a familiar part of a Maui beach scene, and even if their masters don't try the water, the dogs will probably find it irresistible.

SOLITUDE AND QUIET BEACHES

Uncrowded shores beckon walkers, swimmers and surfers, picnickers, and those who simply like to watch the sea.

... BEACHES

AMONG THE MOST PICTURESQUE *of the island's beaches, the palm-fringed* *crescent of sand at Kapalua Bay, below, is a photographer's delight.*

GLENN CHRISTIANSEN

TOM TRACY

SURFERS' FAVORITE is Honolua Bay, above. The long row of Norfolk Island pines lines the road to Pineapple Hill. Picnic over, the group at left waits patiently for that famous Maui sunset. Clouds that gather over Lanai, Molokai, and Kahoolawe make West Maui's sunsets among the best in the islands.

CANE FIELDS SLOPE TO THE MOUNTAINS

A food crop of the early
Polynesians is now Hawaii's most
important agricultural product.

*FIELDS OF RIPPLING SUGAR CANE
cloak the foothills and plains of
central and western Maui. Brought to
Hawaii in the canoes of the first
arrivals, sugar cane was growing wild
when Captain Cook arrived in 1778.
Now it is a major crop on the four
largest islands. All but about three
per cent of the sugar produced in
Hawaii is shipped raw for processing
on the mainland.*

148

. . . CANE FIELDS

CANE PLANTING still occasionally uses techniques from the past, though the industry today is highly mechanized. At some fields, such as these near Puunene, seed cane is hand cut, fill-in planting is done by hand after an initial planting by machine, and mules are sometimes used to carry seed cane to the planting crew. Harvesting begins with spectacular burning of field — usually at night or in early morning when winds are quiet. The fire removes dry leaves, leaving the juice-filled stalks, which are loaded onto enormous cane-hauling trucks and carried to mill for processing. Cane takes eighteen to twenty-four months to ripen.

PHOTOGRAPHS BY BOONE MORRISON

WEST MAUI . . . HISTORY, SHOPPING, RESORTS

A tourist playground thrives on a coast visited by kings,
missionaries, and whalers in earlier times.

*A SAILORS' BRIG in whaling
days, Hale Paahao has been
refurbished and is open to
visitors. Inside the compound is
a cell block with ten lock-ups.*

*NEW ENGLAND-STYLE Baldwin Home, now a museum, was the home of medical missionary
Dwight Baldwin from 1836 to 1868. Walls are of plastered coral, beams are hand-hewn ohia.*

PIONEER INN, now renovated and expanded, is still a popular place from which to watch the passing scene. Hotel dates from 1901, and house rules of that time are posted in its rooms. In barroom, shipping lists detail cargoes and tonnages of whaling ships that called at Lahaina in 1843. Original part of hotel is at far left in photograph, recent addition of shops with rooms above is in foreground.

SUPER WHALE
clothes for children

Holiday Shop

THE SHOPPING SCENE in Lahaina is a varied one, with assorted items displayed in old buildings, refurbished ones, and brand new quarters designed to be compatible with their older surroundings.

BOONE MORRISON

A WHALE MOTIF is featured throughout the Whalers Village complex, where specialty shops and restaurants ramble over eight acres of the Kaanapali resort community north of Lahaina.

TOM TRACY

THE CARTHAGINIAN, three-masted Danish schooner that once sailed the Baltic Sea, was transformed into a whaling squarerigger for the film "Hawaii." Now she is a whaling museum and a romantic addition to Lahaina's waterfront scene.

EDITOR'S NOTE: As we were going to press, the Carthaginian hit a reef while being taken to drydock, and was damaged beyond repair.

A. SALBOSA

BUILT TO 1890-1910 VINTAGE, train of Lahaina Kaanapali & Pacific Railroad chugs along on narrow-gauge tracks from outskirts of Lahaina to depot near Kaanapali hotels. Its steam engine incorporates parts of five early Hawaiian locomotives.

BEAUTIFULLY MANICURED golf greens and gardens surround the resort hotels and condominiums that stretch from the sea to the lower slopes of the West Maui Mountains at Kaanapali. Here luxurious hotels offer complete resort facilities, and visitors can stroll the sun-warmed sands of one of the Islands' longest and loveliest beaches.

A THREE-MILE-LONG BEACH of wave-smoothed sand fronts hotels and golf course and is a major Kaanapali attraction.

EAST MAUI'S JUNGLED COAST

Unforgettable beauty appears at every turn of the road, a special magic surrounds a quiet, unspoiled bit of Hawaii, and a native wilderness is preserved in an isolated section of a national park.

KEITH GUNNAR

A CRISP, FRESH-WATER POOL is hidden away in this lava tube at Waianapanapa State Park. Hawaiians say the pool water turns red in spring, supposedly with the blood of a legendary princess said to have been killed here by her jealous lover.

TWISTING AND DEMANDING, but a worthwhile adventure, the road to Hana coils along a sea-lashed coast, clinging to forested cliffs, burrowing into gulches draped with waterfalls, and crossing streams on narrow concrete bridges that date back more than half a century.

161

...EAST MAUI

WAILUA FALLS cascades down Haleakala's wet windward slope and pours over a jungled cliff to enter the sea at Wailua Cove. Between Hana and Kipahulu, the road winds in and out of Wailua Gulch, past two impressive waterfalls, through a forest of gnarled kukui, and beneath slopes that are a tangle of tropical foliage.

KEANAE PENINSULA is a picturesque patchwork of green taro fields and tiny gardens. A spur road from the Hana "highway" leads down to the quiet settlement where people work the swampy plots and fish from a foam-splashed shore. The coral stone church at left is more than one hundred years old.

MAUI **163**

HALEAKALA NATIONAL PARK sweeps from the 10,023-foot summit of the mountain down to the East Maui shore. Its splendid seaward addition includes beautiful Kipahulu Valley and its Seven Pools, lovely chain of waterfalls and swimming holes that topple into one another from above the road bridge all the way to the sea.

BOONE MORRISON

GLISTENING BLACK STONES heaped on this beach at the edge of Hana Bay
are constantly tumbled and rattled about by a sea that is sometimes gentle,
sometimes tumultuous. In the photograph above, their smooth, wet surfaces reflect
the glow of an early morning sunrise.

HALEAKALA . . . FERTILE SLOPES AND A VAST CRATER

The air is bracing, the views magnificent, and crops and cattle flourish
on the upper slopes of this mighty volcano, which last erupted about 1790.

TOM TRACY

TOM TRACY

UP ON THE COOL SLOPES
of Haleakala, fragrant groves
of eucalyptus shade the road,
fat cattle look up from lush
pastures that overlook the sea,
and farmers grow flowers and
vegetables, including most of
the state's cabbage crop.

MAUI **167**

MAUI'S LARGEST RANCH began life as a sugar cane plantation under the ownership of former whaling captain James Makee. Lawns and gardens, lovely old trees, and gentle grazing land surround the rambling frame ranch house above, built by the captain in 1857. On a hill nearby are the ruins of the Makee mill and a signal gun the captain fired to welcome arriving ships.

BOONE MORRISON

PORTUGUESE IMMIGRANTS were among the settlers who farmed the productive fields of Maui's Kula district in the 1800's and were the original parishers of the quaint octagonal Catholic Church of the Holy Ghost built in 1897 on Old Kula Road high on the tranquil slopes of the mountain. The church altar was made in Austria and shipped in sections around Cape Horn.

SUBTLY TINTED symmetrical cones rise from a painted wasteland within Haleakala, "house of the sun." According to legend, Maui, the prankster demigod, once snared the sun from the rim of this volcano and slowed it in its race across the sky so that his mother would have more time to dry her kapa. The rare silversword plant, left, is protected here. It takes seven to twenty years for the famous plant to bloom. Then a single flower stalk rises three to eight feet from the silvery leaf cluster, blooms for one short season, from June through October, forms seeds, and dies.

PHOTOGRAPHS BY ROBERT WENKAM (THIS PAGE), DAVID MUENCH (OPPOSITE)

THE NENE, Hawaii's state bird, was once almost extinct. From an estimated population of 25,000 during the late 1800's, their number dwindled to less than 50 by 1945. A restoration program supported by private donors, wildlife societies, and government grants has brought the nene population up to about 600 birds. Birds are raised at Pohakuloa breeding station on the Big Island's Saddle Road. Release site on Maui is at Paliku, at the east end of the crater.

. . . HALEAKALA

MAUNA KEA AND MAUNA LOA on the Big Island show their snow-tipped peaks above the clouds that hang low over Alenuihaha Channel in view at left from Haleakala. Above, quaint Hui Aloha Church has occupied this grassy peninsula at Kaupo for more than one hundred years.

MAUI **173**

Kauai

Kauai, the Garden Island, combines razor-sharp ridges, deep canyons, jungled valleys, and white sand beaches. Scattered among its natural scenic beauties are fields of sugar cane and pineapple, taro patches, quiet towns, and resort clusters. This is the oldest of the major islands in the Hawaiian chain, and it was the first to be visited by Captain Cook. It was the only one of the group to submit voluntarily to the all-island rule of Kamehameha the Great. At the island's center are the wet, forested slopes of Waialeale, the ancient volcano that built Kauai. Low-hanging clouds usually obscure its highest peak, Kawaikini, which, with an average rainfall of over four hundred inches a year, is said to be the wettest place on earth. In the high, cool, mountain heartland of the island, an untamed back country laced by trails overlooks some of Hawaii's most spectacular scenery. Around the edges, tropical foliage shades sandy curves of beach, and surf crashes relentlessly against jagged lava. The northwest coast is a series of magnificent roadless valleys where waterfalls drop over verdant cliffs and streams thread their way through a jungled landscape to the sea.

PHOTOGRAPH BY BOONE MORRISON

A LUXURIANT LANDSCAPE SURROUNDS A WET SUMMIT

Lush vegetation almost blankets this greenest island in the chain, and a scenic wonderland extends downward from Kauai's rain-soaked heartland.

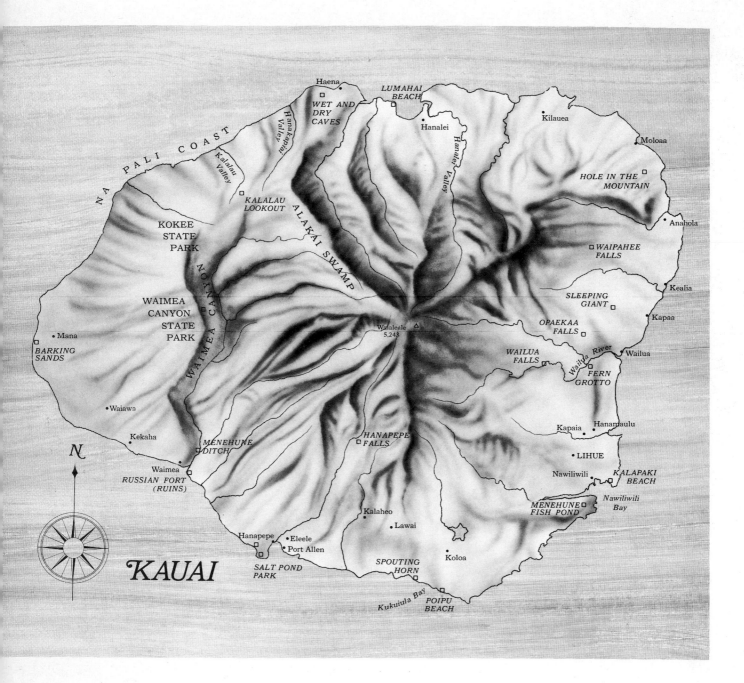

WAILUA RIVER excursion to celebrated Fern Grotto is on the itinerary of most Kauai visitors. For three miles, the tour boats chug upriver into beautiful back country.

DAVID MUENCH

... A LUXURIANT LANDSCAPE

LUSHNESS AND VARIETY of its natural vegetation have earned Kauai the nickname "the Garden Island." Plant material varies from that found in the cool, misty, high altitudes to lush tropical jungle and some outstanding cultivated collections.

WAIALEALE'S SUMMIT is usually obscured by low-hanging clouds that drop torrential rains of 400 to 600 inches a year atop the ancient volcano. Streams rush seaward through verdant valleys eroded in Waialeale's green forested flanks.

KAUAI **179**

OHIA LEHUA tree is seen throughout the Islands and grows especially well on cool, higher slopes, as here above Kalalau Valley. In early Hawaii, its feathery, red blossoms were considered sacred. Hawaiian chiefs made leis of them for Pele, the volcano goddess. Today leaves, seed pods, buds, and blossoms are used for leis.

. . . A LUXURIANT LANDSCAPE

REMOTE ALAKAI SWAMP, high on the western shoulder of Waialeale, is so nearly level that rainfall soaks it thoroughly before dropping from the plateau in mighty waterfalls. Alakai's approximately fifteen square miles are a botanical treasure house of native flora.

NA PALI... BOLD PRECIPICES HIDE MAGNIFICENT VALLEYS

Between razor-sharp ridges of the spectacular northwest coast, deep, jungled valleys that cut inland from the sea hold a wealth of opportunities for outdoorsmen.

NANCY BANNICK

MASSIVE LAVA CLIFFS rise 2,000 to 3,000 feet from the surf that pounds against the Na Pali Coast. When the sea calms in summer, sandy beaches appear at the seaward ends of deep, jungled valleys. A steep but easy two-mile trail from road's end near Haena leads into Hanakapiai Valley, above.

DAVID MUENCH

. . . NA PALI

DESERTED BEACHES such as Kalalau, above, nestle beneath towering black lava cliffs, and green-clad bluffs slope steeply to the sea. Still relatively inaccessible, though helicopter excursions now provide easier access, the remote valleys of Kauai's northwest shore are still a world for hikers.

PHOTOGRAPHS BY ROBERT WENKAM

*TARO GROWS WILD beneath
gnarled kukui trees and alongside
Nualolo Stream, which tumbles
through a valley inhabited long ago
by early Hawaiians who cultivated
their plants on stone-walled terraces
and irrigated them with water
diverted from the stream.*

A SOUTH SEAS SETTING ON THE NORTH SHORE

Pandanus-laden cliffs edge quiet coves, and precipitous green mountains
rise behind a peaceful valley checkered with patches of taro.

BOONE MORRISON

*A QUIET HARBOR greets sailors at Hanalei Bay. Biennially,
boats race from Honolulu to Hanalei following the
Transpacific Yacht Race from the mainland. At right,
pandanus frames a view of lovely Lumahai Beach, one of
the most photographed beaches in the Islands.*

DAVID MUENCH

BELOW KUHIO HIGHWAY, the Hanalei Valley, above and right, is a patchwork of emerald-green taro patches cut by the silvery Hanalei River, which threads its way down from the forested mountains.

HEART-SHAPED LEAVES of taro plants stretch back to jagged green peaks set off against a blue, blue sky. Kauai grows the most taro of all the islands. Poi is made by cooking and pounding the heavy roots.

KAUAI **189**

HOLE IN THE MOUNTAIN, at right of jagged peak in center of photograph, is said to have been made when a great chief threw his spear with such force that it went right through this mountain ridge near Anahola.

LEGENDS LIVE ON IN THE ISLAND LANDSCAPE

Industrious elves and powerful chiefs performed prodigious feats in the legends of Kauai, and evidences of their accomplishments play a prominent role in today's tale-telling.

WILLIAM SOLLNER

BUILT BY THE MENEHUNE, Alakoko Fishpond is one example of the many works attributed to this mysterious race of shy little people who worked only at night to build dams, ditches, paved trails, and other unexplained stonework seen on Kauai.

KAUAI'S CASCADES ARE SOMETHING SPECIAL

Magnificent waterfalls drop from high, verdant cliffs, and summit rainfall sends full streams rushing down Waialeale's slopes.

TOM TRACY

RIBBONS OF WATER plunge over canyon walls into pools banked with greenery. Wailua Falls, above, is a rushing torrent after a heavy rainfall. At right, Opaekaa Falls drops in a lacy pattern of silver over dark lava cliffs.

DAVID MUENCH

REFRESHING STREAMS tumble down Waialeale's wet slopes and follow boulder-strewn courses to the sea. Above is Hanakapiai Stream on the Na Pali Coast.

WILLIAM SOLLNER

*RIDING A WATERFALL is great sport, and Waipahee Falls' natural rock slide is a
local favorite. It was reproduced in concrete in Kilauea Stream for the film "South Pacific."*　**195**

A PARKLAND OF UNFORGETTABLE BEAUTY

In two state parks high on Kauai's western slopes, a beautiful, untrampled back country, laced with trails for strollers and hikers, overlooks some of Hawaii's most spectacular scenery.

BOONE MORRISON

THE WAIMEA RIVER has sliced a miniature Grand Canyon through the lava slopes. Reds, browns, and greens subtly color the 2,857-foot-deep gorge in a palette that constantly changes with the shifting cloud shadows. Above, tangled koas edge a grassy clearing in Kokee State Park.

REEF-PROTECTED BAYS on the south shore lure swimmers and skin divers. Youngsters paddle about endlessly in the calm, shallow waters off Poipu Beach, above, and Salt Pond Park, right. The latter is named for salt beds nearby, where coarse salt is still made in the manner of the early Hawaiians.

SHELTERED COVES AND WAVE-WASHED SHORES

Offshore reefs still the waters in idyllic coves, while not far away, surf splashes over rocky points, and waves formed far out in the open sea break uninterrupted on long, smooth stretches of sandy beach.

THE SEA PUSHES UP through a shoreline lava tube at the Spouting Horn. According to local legend, the sorrowful moaning sound heard each time a geyser shoots skyward is the crying of an unhappy lizard trapped in the tube below.

KAUAI **199**

BOONE MORRISON

...WAVE-WASHED SHORES

THE OPEN SEA is a vast, empty expanse that stretches endlessly outward from an undisturbed shore between Kekaha and Mana in views broken only by the outline of tiny Niihau island, which hugs the horizon in the sunset scene above.

Molokai

Tourism is just beginning to touch the Friendly Isle. New residential and resort areas are under development, but most of Molokai is still a rural landscape of pineapple fields, ranches, and small farms. The island was formed by two major volcanic domes. The tableland called Mauna Loa at the western end, which rises to only 1,381 feet, was the first to build up. The jagged mountains in the northeast, topped by 4,940-foot Kamakou, were formed later by the East Molokai volcano. A much younger volcano, Kauhako, created a flat tongue of land that juts out from the north coast, isolated from the rest of the island by fortress-like cliffs. Sufferers of leprosy were exiled there for almost a century, and the settlement of Kalaupapa is still home for some recovered patients who have chosen to remain. Molokai has many attractions for outdoorsmen. Campers can choose from beautiful sites in mountain meadows, on the banks of sparkling streams, and along the ocean's edge. Hikers can explore green-carpeted valleys where Hawaiian taro farmers and fishermen once lived and where bananas, mangoes, sugar cane, taro, and ginger grow wild and waterfalls drop from towering cliffs. Hunters can go after deer, goats, wild boar, and game birds, and the submarine shelf that juts twenty-seven miles into the sea from the island's southwest corner is one of Hawaii's most fertile fishing grounds.

PHOTOGRAPH BY BOONE MORRISON

PLANTATION TOWNS AND OLD HAWAII

Pineapple fields and pasture lands cover much of this tranquil,
unexploited island, still bypassed by most Island visitors.

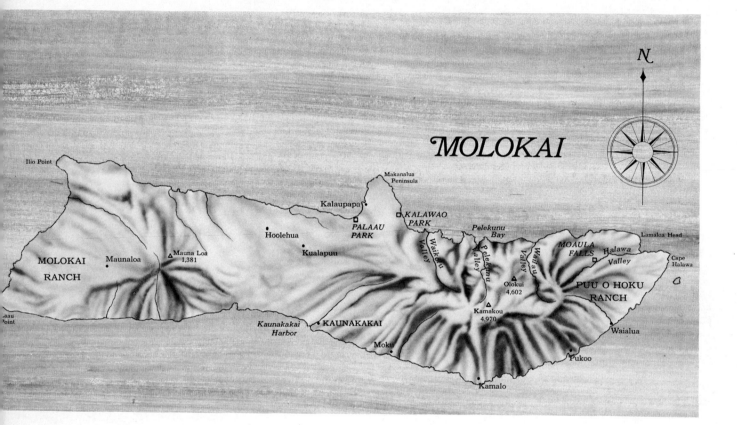

*PLANTED BY KAMEHAMEHA V
more than a hundred years ago,
coconut trees in this extensive
grove near Kaunakakai now
shade a shoreside park enjoyed
by picnickers of today.*

BOONE MORRISON

... PLANTATION TOWNS

KALOHI CHANNEL, viewed below from the hills overlooking Kaunakakai, is a
calm, protected passage between islands. Some nine miles away, the
north coast of Lanai looms up across the water. Pineapple fields cover much of western
Molokai. Headquarters for the plantation is Maunaloa, left, where the rooftops
of employees' homes hug a hillside above precisely patterned fields.

BOONE MORRISON

A DEVOTED PRIEST SERVED A LONELY SETTLEMENT

Strangers are welcome now on the tiny peninsula that was a place of banishment for almost a century, and Molokai, once called the Lonely Isle, is now the Friendly Isle.

THE VIEW FROM PALAAU PARK, above, shows the reason for Kalaupapa's name, which translates "the leafy plain." The colony lies on a flat peninsula beneath fortress-like cliffs, which served to isolate victims of leprosy from 1866 until sulfone drugs were discovered in 1946. In the cemetery of St. Philomena Church (right), a monument honors Father Damien, who lived with the victims from 1873 until he died of the disease in 1889.

DAVID CORNWELL

ROADLESS VALLEYS NOTCH THE SHORE

Dropping away from steep mountains topped by 4,970-foot-high
Kamakou, wet valleys edge the windward side of East Molokai
and dry gulches slice deep into the hills above the southern shore.

BOONE MORRISON

WET WAIKOLU VALLEY supplies water,.via a five-mile tunnel, to Molokai's thirsty western plains.

DRY KAUNAKAKAI GULCH, on the island's lee side, burrows deep into the slopes behind the town.

...ROADLESS VALLEYS

AT THE EASTERN TIP of the island, green-carpeted Halawa Valley reaches the sea at this rock-edged cove. Inland, gorgeous jungle scenery rewards the hiker and remains of old irrigation ditches and terraced taro patches are reminders of the days when hundreds of people lived in these beautiful surroundings. The now-deserted church at left was built more than a century ago as a branch of Kaluaaha mission.

Lanai

This small island, just a half hour by air from Honolulu, is most known for pineapples, and pineapples do indeed cover acres and acres of Lanai's slopes. But for those who find pleasure in quiet surroundings and who like to explore little-traveled, undeveloped shores, Lanai has more than pineapples to offer. The island is the remains of an old volcanic peak that rises to more than 3,000 feet at its high point, Lanaihale. On the west side, a cultivated plateau ends in jagged cliffs that drop off to the sea. On the windward side, luxuriant gulches slope to a half-mile-wide coastal plain where reef-protected shoals offer good spear and net fishing, deserted shores reward beachcombers, and remains of old Hawaiian villages wait to be explored. Lanai has cool, forested mountains with pleasant hiking trails; grassy knolls on rolling hillsides are ideal picnic sites, with fine views over the slopes and across the water to other islands; and Lanai's weathered boulders bear some of Hawaii's best petroglyphs.

PHOTOGRAPH BY NANCY BANNICK

PINEAPPLES AND QUIET BEAUTY

This small island claims to be the "world's largest pineapple plantation." More than 15,000 acres are planted in pineapples, the Islands' second largest agricultural crop.

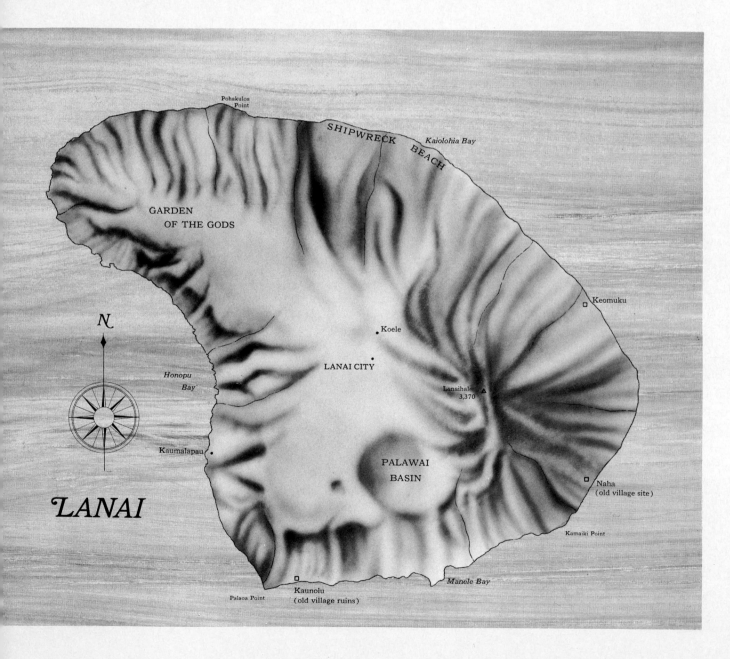

Pohakuloa Point

SHIPWRECK BEACH

Kaiolohia Bay

GARDEN OF THE GODS

Keomuku

N

Koele

Honopu Bay

LANAI CITY

Lanaihale 3,370

Kaumalapau

PALAWAI BASIN

Naha (old village site)

LANAI

Kamaiki Point

Manele Bay

Palaoa Point

Kaunolu (old village ruins)

THE SUN SPARKLES on the sheltered waterway between Lanai and Maui where whaleships anchored in the 1800's and where winter season whale-watching is a popular pastime today.

. . . PINEAPPLES

NEW CROP grows from crowns cut from previously harvested pineapples. Crowns are planted by hand through strips of plastic, which control moisture, warm the soil, keep down weeds. Crop is hand-harvested after about 21 months by a crew that picks the ripened fruit, removes the tops, and drops both tops and fruit onto conveyor belt of harvesting machine. The tops are saved for a future planting.

GIGANTIC, TWO-ARMED sprinkler drags its own water supply hose behind. Below, crates of ripe pineapple are loaded onto waiting barges at Kaumalapau Harbor for shipment to cannery in Honolulu.

PHOTOGRAPHS BY BOONE MORRISON

REMINDERS OF THE PAST

Remnants of old Hawaii and evidence of people long since gone still survive on Lanai's little-traveled shores.

PETROGLYPHS at Kukui Point were discovered just a few years ago. Large rounded boulders like these were a favored surface for this early artwork.

IN AN OASIS OF PALM TREES on the sandy windward coast, Keomuku village is a ghost town of a few old houses and this weathered church.

THE CONTRASTS ARE GREAT

On the eastern slopes, ridges are forested, gulches clad in green; across the island, a pineapple and scrub-covered plateau ends in cliffs above the sea.

DEEP RAVINES furrow Lanai's windward coast. Maunalei Gulch, right, cuts a swath to the sea below Hookio Ridge. From the top of the island, at 3,370 feet, all of the major islands except Kauai come into view on a clear day. The view from Lanaihale's eastern slope, below, is across Auau Channel to the West Maui Mountains.

BOONE MORRISON

BOONE MORRISON

BOONE MORRISON

ANSEL ADAMS

*A RAIN FOREST OF FERNS
and other tropicals on
Lanaihale, left, contrasts
strikingly with the arid,
uncultivated northwestern
plateau, above. Norfolk
Island pines were planted
many years ago to increase
Lanai's ground water—
weather studies show that
the trees collect moisture
from hill-hugging clouds.
The dirt road above winds
through Garden of the Gods,
a color-tinged canyon of
windswept sand strewn with
lava boulders, shaped and
eroded by the elements.*

This book was printed and bound by Kingsport Press, Kingsport, Tennessee, from litho film prepared by Graphic Arts Center, Portland, Oregon. Body type is Optima composed by Atherton's Advertising Typography, Palo Alto, California. Type for heads is Studio photocomposed by Reprotype, San Francisco. Paper for pages is Mountie Enamel made by Northwest Paper Co., Cloquet, Minnesota.